YOUTH
DOES
STILL SPEAK?

YOUTH FORUM SERIES

Titles in Print

YOUTH FORUM SERIES

Youth Asks,
DOES GOD
STILL SPEAK?

by

Andrew M. Greeley

THOMAS NELSON INC.
CAMDEN, NEW JERSEY

Library of Congress Catalog Card Number: 72-110140

Printed in the United States of America

For
Rich Mortell
who faced the issue.

Foreword

Written in the context of the Christian faith, this book is one in a series published by Thomas Nelson Inc. in collaboration with Youth Research Center.

The research agency, which serves as editor of this series, is known through *What Youth Are Thinking* (Smedsrud, 1961) and *Profiles of Church Youth* (Strommen, 1963). The Director, Dr. Merton Strommen, is known also for his work as Director of Research (1965-67) with Religious Education Association, an inter-faith agency serving all church groups.

The purpose of the series is to use points of established need to bring about meaningful contact between the GOSPEL of God in Jesus Christ and YOUNG PEOPLE. Underlying the total effort is a concern that youth throughout the English-speaking world can be helped to see that the Gospel of Christ is the core of life itself in all its realities.

Unique to this publication effort is the use that is made of research findings. These describe the specific need to which each book is addressed as well as the youth most concerned about this need. Thus a writer is helped to speak more directly to the actual conflicts, values, and beliefs of an important segment of youth.

The significance of this series is enhanced by the scholarship and pastoral concern of the authors. Their grasp of the fields in which each writes enables them to speak with authority, establishing the series as a basic reference in the area of youth work.

Preface

Just at the time when, after snubbing each other for 400 years or so, Roman Catholics and Protestants finally resumed the conversation that had been so rudely interrupted, they suddenly discovered that no one was really listening.

In the sixteenth century the two sides debated about whether or not there was any justification for addressing prayers to the saints; today the problem is whether or not there is any point in addressing prayers to God. Then they argued about the Immaculate Conception of the Virgin Mary, the Mother of God; now the question is the Virgin Birth of Christ, the Son of God, or indeed the divine Sonship of Christ, or, for that matter, the divine Fatherhood of God.

There is, therefore, a neat irony in the invitation that a Lutheran historian of theology write a foreword for a brief volume by a Roman Catholic sociologist. It could, of course, be justified on various grounds: Father Greeley is a Ph.D. alumnus of the University of Chicago and a member of its staff, I am also a Ph.D. alumnus of the University of Chicago and was, from 1953 to 1962, a member of its faculty. As a social scientist concerned in his research with public opinion, Father Greeley cannot avoid history, although social scientists sometimes try; as a historian concerned chiefly with the public opinion of the dead, I cannot avoid the implications of social science, although there are times when I wish I could.

Yet none of these can qualify as the principal reason for my accepting this assignment. The chief justification for my doing this job for such a book as this by an author of the caliber of Andrew Greeley is that both he and I and, I hope, most of the readers of this book have something very fundamental in common. We find ourselves in the position of not being able either to accept unequivocally or to deny categorically the view of God which we have inherited from our past tradition. We may envy those who can still accept it unequivocally, though we may also suspect them; we may respect those who deny it categorically, though we may also wonder whether they are as cocksure in their atheism as they seem. But we find ourselves living between the two worlds.

This is not to say that, in the final analysis, either Father Greeley or I would regard the question of God as one that can be left in suspension. If it is as vital as, by its very definition, it claims to be, any answer is better than no answer. "He that is not with me is against me," an Authority whom we would all acknowledge has declared. But it does mean that the easy assistance which faith in God used to receive from its non-churchly environment is a source of support upon which believers may no longer rely—and that, in at least some ways, this is a plus for those believers. So long as believing in God was a part of the etiquette of society and only the drugstore atheist raised questions about it, Christians could (and did) cheat in their faith.

Today it is no longer obligatory, nor even fashionable, to believe in God. And therefore believing in God has come to matter as it did not when belief was a matter of the current fad. Father Greeley's essay does not try to show that it is easy or obvious or popular to affirm the reality of God. It does maintain that anyone who avoids the issue is not only evading the fundamental implications of the nature of being, but is depriving himself of a vital resource for understanding the ambiguity and the promise within the continuing tragedy of human life.

Thus it may well be that, even in an age when atheism is more influential than ecumenism, the voice of a churchman who is a scholar in a university, complemented by the voice of another churchman who is a scholar in another university, will speak a word of meaning and power to a generation of youth who are truly ready to "face the issue."

Jaroslav Pelikan
Yale University

Contents

13

the death of God

Have you not heard of that madman who lit a lantern in the bright morning hours, ran to the market place, and cried incessantly, "I seek God! I seek God!" As many of those who do not believe in God were standing around just then, he provoked much laughter. . . .

"Whither is God" he cried. "I shall tell you. *We have killed him*—you and I. All of us are his murderers. But how have we done this? How were we able to drink up the sea? Who gave us the sponge to wipe away the entire horizon? What did we do when we unchained this earth from its sun? Whither is it moving now? Whither are we moving now? Away from all suns? Are we not plunging continually?. . . . Do we not hear anything yet of the noise of the gravediggers who are burying God? Do we not smell anything yet of God's decomposition? Gods too decompose. God is dead. . . . Is not the greatness of this deed too great for us? Must not we ourselves become gods simply to seem worthy of it? There has never been a greater deed; and whoever will be born after us—for the sake of this deed he will be part of a higher history than all history hitherto."

. . . It has been related further that on the same day the madman entered divers churches and there sang his *requiem aeternam deo*. Led out and called to account, he is said to have replied each time, "What are these churches now if they are not the tombs and sepulchers of God?" [1]

Thus did Friedrich Nietzsche rather melodramatically announce the death of God. The science and the wisdom, the enlightenment and the skepticism of the nineteenth century had at last disposed of God and man could finally be free.

What is surprising is not so much the arrogance of Nietzsche or of his twentieth-century followers, who have perhaps more of a public relations flare than Nietzsche did, but their naïveté, and what is surprising about their naïveté is not that they think they can persuade the vast majority of men that God is dead, but rather that they think they are the first who have tried to kill Him; that they are the first of the skeptics, the first of the agnostics, the first of the atheists; that now for the first time man is so wise that he no longer needs to seek God to find an explanation for life. It is a naïveté based on the odd notion that science makes the act of commitment more difficult than it has been before, and that it introduces doubt and skepticism into

[1] From *The Gay Science* in *The Portable Nietzsche* (pages 95-6) translated and edited by Walter Kaufmann, copyright 1954 by the Viking Press. Used by permission.

the act of faith that was not there previously. Now that we have perfectly natural explanations of lightning and thunder, of flood and hurricane, of birth, growth, and death, the problem of the rationality and the graciousness of the universe is somehow or other less puzzling and less insistent than it was before. It is also a naïveté which brings the strange belief that dissatisfactions with the attempts of human language to speak about the gods was something which began only shortly before Bishop John Robinson wrote his book, *Honest to God.*[2] It is, finally, a strange naïveté which thinks that the freedom man purchases when the gods die comes any more easily in an age of science than it did in an age of myth.

In every generation and in every culture there are those who would, in one fashion or another, announce the death of God. The primitive man is no less a skeptic than modern man, though his skepticism may take very different forms. Every age, every culture, every human being must wrestle with the God question. And the negative answer, while it has always been the minority response, has always been made. For modern man the God question is more difficult, not so much because of the findings of science, but because the obstacles and the irrelevancies that stand in the way of a clear decision about God—indeed, even in the way of a clear statement of the issue—are much more serious than they have been in the past and because half answers and refusals to face the question have, for the first time in human history, become fashionable. Men have

[2] Philadelphia: Westminster Press, 1963.

answered "Yes" or "No" for countless ages to the question, "Is God dead?" but our modern age is the first one to produce a large number of people who shrug their shoulders and say "Maybe."

It is not the purpose of this book to answer the question of whether God is dead. Ultimately every man must answer this question for himself in the light of his own religious tradition and experience and through the act of faith in the existence or nonexistence of God (to put the issue in terms which are something less than adequate.) Nor will we attempt in any detail to provide answers to the questions of "If there is a God, who is He and what is He," because long before these questions can be asked, man must decide first that "He is." We will attempt, rather, to provide the raw material from which an answer to the God question may be fashioned, and to indicate what the issue really is and how the question ought to be asked. Our work, therefore, is essentially the work of clearing away obstacles and disposing of irrelevancies that stand in the way of wrestling with God much the same way that Jacob wrestled with his angel.

We may be sure that we are not the first who have so wrestled. The shepherd sitting on the hillside watching the stars, the Egyptian priest studying the movements of the sun and the rise and flow of the Nile, the cave man staring into his fire, Plato dreaming of his caves, Aristotle pouring over his syllogisms, Anselm in the dusty library of his medieval monastery, Kierkegaard staring out of his lonely apartment on the rainy streets of Copenhagen, Camus on the sands of the Mediterranean walked once before by Augustine— these are but the great names of the men who pondered the mystery of God. All of us in the human condition have had to answer the question, though some of us have answered it routinely and with little agony. But in the modern world, for weal or woe, easy answers to the God question are no longer possible and most young people cannot escape with the relatively unpainful acceptance of the faith of their ancestors. Man has always had to decide for himself; in our day man must decide explicitly and consciously, and, at times painfully. Is there, indeed, a transcendent reality that we cover with the label "God," and if there is, what does this mean for our lives?

But if the question is more conscious and explicit in our day for more people, it does not really mean that the question is any different than it has been in the past. As we shall attempt to suggest in this volume, the problem is not merely that we are skeptical about the nonmaterial, the supernatural, the nonempirical; of course we are, and the nineteenth-century positivists did not introduce this skepticism into the human condition. Immersed in matter as he is, man doubts the existence of anything that transcends the material; the positivist who says that he can admit the existence only of that which he can empirically verify is simply stating in somewhat more elevated language the inclination that has been part of the historic human condition.

The problem with the God question is more serious

not simply because of the fact that God is empirically
unverifiable, though admittedly if there was some way
we could verify Him empirically, it might ease the issue
somewhat. The problem is rather more subtle. It is that
God is too good to be true, for to believe in Him is not
even fundamentally to affirm the existence of some
transcendental personage, but it is to affirm far more;
belief in God involves a commitment to goodness, to belief in the rationality and graciousness of the universe,
to the belief that somehow or other there is purpose in
life beyond life itself. And this faith, this commitment,
runs against the grain of human skepticism far more
fiercely than does the existence of a personage who may
either be Aristotle's unmoved ruler or a kindly old
gentleman in the sky, or anything in between, including Paul Tillich's *Ground of Being.*[3]

It is possible, of course, to believe in the goodness,
rationality, and graciousness of reality and not believe
in a "personal" God, though the problem here is generally semantic rather than theological. It is also possible
to believe in God and to have only the vaguest notions
of the possibility of transcendence and of life beyond
life. This possibility seems to be a rare one in the Western cultural tradition. To affirm God, therefore, is to
affirm purpose and goodness in life which transcends—
goes beyond—life itself; and even if this affirmation
only very vaguely addresses itself to the possibility of
personal life after death, it is still so glorious and aston-

[3] Tillich somewhere or other confesses that he would much have
preferred to use the term *ipsum esse,* but that unfortunately Thomas
Aquinas had beaten him to the term.

ishing that man's suspicions, distrust, and fear incline him to be dubious. He cannot, in the strict sense of the word, empirically validate the graciousness or non-graciousness of reality. He must make a commitment to one position or another. He must make an act of faith in rationality and goodness or in evil and chaos; man somehow or other frequently thinks that it is more intelligent, more mature, and safer to believe in chaos because then he does not run the risk of expecting too much; he does not run the risk of being "chumped"; he does not run the risk of being naïve or foolish or innocent. It is the hard, cynical, sophisticated dimension of the human personality that inclines man to say, "None of it's true," while it is the innocent, open, fresh, and optimistic strains within human nature that incline man to say, "Perhaps it is true."

The God issue, then, has nothing to do with science and nothing to do with empirical validation; it has nothing to do ultimately with the language we use or the childhood images we have of the great Santa Claus or, alternately, the Great Hangman of the Sky. It has nothing to do even with the question of whether God is a person, a question that is almost unanswerable, considering the multitude of meanings given to the word "person." Rather, the God issue ultimately comes to whether man is able to decide that there is rationality and graciousness in the world around him, rationality and graciousness that cannot be explained by sheer chance. If there is, then man can afford to be hopeful. And if there is not, no matter what brave front

he may put on it, no matter how much he may hide
from the harshness of reality, there is nothing left for
man but despair.

The atheist and, as we shall see in the next chapter,
the agnostic, claim that their decision is a courageous
one and that those who believe in God do so because
they lack the bravery and the heroism to face unafraid
a meaningless existence. Whether hope or despair requires more courage seems, however, to be a quite ir-
relevant question. Both acts require a leap beyond the
available empirical evidence. Both require commitment of the personality. Both involve overcoming the
fear that one may be wrong. Both involve faith. It is
the nature of the human condition that man cannot
fashion an explanation for reality without faith, whether
the explanation affirms rationality and graciousness or
denies it.

It is worth noting, as one embarks on a journey
toward the solution of the God issue, that most men do
indeed believe in God; there is little evidence that the
atheist or secularist theologians have found many dis-
ciples or are likely to find very many. One does not, of
course, arrive at religious or moral truth by taking public opinion polls, although some of the secularist theologians seem to be inclined to arrive at ethical truth if not
doctrinal truth in this fashion. The secularists are in a
rather awkward position when faced with man's overwhelming belief in God. Most of them are firmly committed to the democratic principles. But the faith in
the masses has to be rather snobbish, for they must as-

sume that the vast majority of the people are ignorant, superstitious, and uneducated and that they,
because of their superior wisdom and education, have
discovered that there is no God and must enlighten the
ignorant masses, an enlightenment that proceeds at a
relatively slow pace. Such a pose is a very uncom-
fortable one for a person who would like to be convinced of his own basically egalitarian and democratic
inclinations.

But even if education does not in itself bring wisdom,
we cannot be satisfied with the majority vote on the
God question; however, neither can the decision of the
majority be completely ignored. In fact, it ought to pre-
dispose us, if not to a favorable decision on the God
question, at least to a realization that the issue is not a
simple one, nor one that can be dismissed with a few
easy answers.

I shall not pretend to be an unbiased explorer in the
search for God with which this book is concerned. No
one who has made up his mind more or less on the
question can hide his own predispositions, and I do not
propose to try. It would be far better, I think, to admit
at the beginning that I do believe in God and that I
fully expect an examination of the "God question" to
end up indicating that a positive response to the question is a valid one. I presume that the young people who
buy this book or who read it would be fully aware that
a Church-sponsored series of booklets would hardly
hire an author who would conclude that faith in God
was invalid. But they should also realize that the be-

liever is no more likely to be biased in his presentation than the unbeliever; that they will find no "neutral" book about God. Once man has made up his mind of the truth or falsehood of the reality, he cannot block out the decision he has made from his consciousness. The only action he can take is to be perfectly honest with those to whom he is speaking and to say what his commitment is. There are no unbiased discussions of the God issue, and young people should beware of someone who claims to be unbiased, because in all likelihood, he is cheating.

But to say that I am biased in favor of the existence of God does not mean that I shall argue dishonestly, or that I will not admit the problems in accepting the reality of God. He who defends political democracy presumably is biased in favor of it, but this bias does not mean either that his arguments are invalid or that political democracy is not a good thing. It simply means that we must watch his arguments with a critical eye to make sure that his biases do not impede their validity. We shall therefore ask the young people who read this book to accept the possibility that I can believe in God and still present an honest case for God's reality, and I shall also ask them to keep a critical eye on my line of reasoning so that they can be sure at the end of the volume that I have not been playing tricks with them.

Perhaps also I should say just a bit about my own experience. I have been a Catholic priest for a decade and a half. I was born, raised, and trained in the pre-Vatican II Catholic Church and find myself enjoying with astonishment the excitement of the post-Vatican II Church, though shifting of gears, intellectual and emotional, that has been necessary in this dramatic change has left me just a little breathless. I spent the first decade of my life as a priest working in a well-to-do Catholic parish (mostly Irish, if the truth be told), in a suburb of Chicago, and whatever its narrowness and limitations—and it had many—this parish was certainly a community of faith where all the social and cultural factors predisposed young people to answer the "God question" positively, which some did after mature and careful thought and others did precipitously and, in my judgment, foolishly. But for the last eight years I have also been in the environment of the University of Chicago, first as a graduate student and then as a member of the staff, and whatever its limitations are at the University of Chicago—and they, too, are many—it could hardly be called a place where religious faith is required and I think, therefore, that my own personal experience has given me an accurate feeling both for the world of faith and for the world of agnosticism. And living in the two worlds as I have, I have been forced to give the agnostic position far more respect than I would have had I never left my pleasant Irish suburb. On the other hand, I have been in the world of agnosticism long enough not to be bemused by its splendors and to realize that while faith has its problems, agnosticism has its problems, too. The young people who read this book may be very correct in saying that neither a well-to-do Irish suburb nor the University of Chicago, individually or collectively, is representative of the typical human experience, but I hope they will grant that if my experiences are not typical, at least they are balanced by their very wide divergencies, and that if I cannot claim to be impartial, I can at least make the more modest claim to be ambivalent.

the agnostic response

We argued in the last chapter that any man who has ever lived has had to wrestle in some fashion, either profoundly or shallowly, with the God question. The normal compromise solution is for man to profess faith in God and to take this faith seriously at certain times in his life, but to behave most of the time as though God did not really matter very much, while keeping in the back of his head the firm intention that, when necessity demanded, he would reach an understanding with God. This sort of compromise was risky, but generally reasonable enough, and has enabled man to enjoy this world and at least have some sort of option on such hereafter as there might be.

But in the last two centuries a different kind of compromise has emerged—the agnostic response to God.

The agnostic responds to the God question (or the God hypothesis, as he chooses to call it) with a shrug of his shoulders. He doesn't know whether there is a God or isn't. He can't prove God's existence, he can't disprove it, and he therefore resolves to live without an answer and with the contention that it doesn't make much difference whether the hypothesis is true or not.

27

The agnostic position, and its positivist philosophical foundation, obtains considerable respectability from its association with positive science which allegedly proceeds on the principle that that which cannot be validated empirically (that is to say, which cannot be measured) cannot be accepted as certainly true. Recent and more sophisticated writings in the philosophy of science, particularly those based on a close study of how great scientists really work, express considerable skepticism as to whether the "positive method" or the "scientific method," as described in the high-school textbooks, in reality has anything to do with the way the scientist operates when he seeks the solution to a problem. Nevertheless, quite simple-minded notions of the meaning of positive science are frequently used to reinforce the agnostic position.

The positivist version of agnosticism runs somewhat as follows: Only that which is empirically verifiable can be accepted as true, but the existence of God is not empirically verifiable; therefore the existence of God cannot be taken to be true. But the nonexistence of God is equally unverifiable, and therefore the nonexistence of God cannot be asserted with confidence, either. God is then a hypothesis. He might exist (though in his heart of hearts the agnostic is inclined to suspect that He doesn't) or He might not exist. But man, bound as he is by the canons of positive validation, really cannot know for sure and has to live without a solution to the question or a confirmation or rejection of the hypothesis.

The positivist will then go on to say that since man really cannot know whether God exists or not, he must find a rationale for his own life within life itself. Self-fulfillment, service, freedom, and other nontranscendental values provide an adequate rationale for human life; and not only is the God hypothesis unverifiable, but more than this, it is unimportant.

One morning several years ago I encountered my friend and colleague, Peter Rossi, in a rather black mood. He had been to a dinner the night before and found himself seated next to a rather liberal clergyman. Given as he is to minor baiting of the clergy, he proceeded to raise the issue of whether it was possible to find a rationale for human life without having recourse to a transcendent reality. The clergyman agreed that it was—that man did not need to postulate a God to find purpose in his own life. Rossi was horrified. This was his own position, of course, but he thought it was most unsporting of the clergyman to agree with him, and also rather shocking that a cleric would espouse an agnostic position. He therefore proceeded for the rest of the evening to argue very strongly that there had to be some purpose of life beyond life itself and to remonstrate with the cleric on his failure to seek out such a purpose and meaning. Even the next morning he was still profoundly scandalized at the clergyman's stand. I pointed out to him that there was some inconsistency in this because the clergyman's stand was no different from his own, but he responded, "I'm not a clergyman, and you guys are supposed to believe in something be-

yond life." And then he added, "Besides, an agnostic
is someone who is afraid there might be a God after
all."

Rossi's half-humorous, half-serious dialogue with the
agnostic cleric illustrates the unease that this half-way
house between theistic faith and atheistic faith generates in a human being. Of the nature of things, the
agnostic cannot be sure; he can't prove there isn't a
God; he is willing to live as though there were no God;
all his scientific training inclines him to think that
there is no God; but there are, nonetheless, rare mo-
ments in his life when he finds himself saying, "My
God, what if I'm wrong?"

It is extraordinarily difficult to discuss ultimate reality, at least, with an agnostic both because the basic
assumptions with which one would enter such a discussion make it impossible for any conclusions to be
achieved, and also because the ambiguity of his position makes him disinclined to discuss the subject. To
quote Peter Rossi once again, "God-talk gives me a
headache."

And yet there are certain observations the believer
must make in response to the agnostic. He must wonder
first of all what kind of a God He would be if He were
empirically verifiable. It is true that certain scientists
with profound faith have been convinced that by the
use of scientific methods they could demonstrate the
existence of God, but such attempts, however sincere
and even passionate, seem rather naïve. By its definition, Transcendental Reality cannot be measured,

cannot be submitted to a microscope or radio telescope or cyclotron. If it could, then it would not be Transcendental Reality. Positive science did not discover that God could not be empirically validated. The authors of the Psalms realized it, too. The positivist assumption adds nothing very new to the God discussion, although it does dress up in more philosophically and scientifically impressive jargon the ancient human inclination to say that if you can't see it, it doesn't exist.

Secondly, one wonders if the agnostic expects mankind to seriously believe that the only form of valid human knowledge is that allegedly acquired in the positive sciences (knowledge which in the years after Einstein and Planck is probabilistic knowledge, in any event). To say that the only valid human knowledge is empirically verifiable knowledge is, in reality, to say that the only kind of knowledge that can be accepted in positive science is empirically verifiable or measurable knowledge, which, in effect, is little more than saying that positive science is positive science. But there clearly are other forms of human understanding, insight, intuition, metaphysics, and faith. The basic asssumption of positivism, that only that which is empirically measurable is valid science, is in itself not an empirically verifiable assumption. And as recent writings in the philosophy of science have made perfectly clear, the scientist is indeed a man of faith even in his own scientific work, because only faith in the rationality and order of reality and the possibility of the human ingenuity expanding its understanding of the operation of this order makes scientific research possible. In Western society we have assumed for several centuries that reality can be understood and that man can systematically progress in such understanding. This assumption is a heroic act of faith which no other culture ever successfully made; and according to some observers, a leap which was made possible only by the religious history of the West.

We therefore find ourselves replying to the agnostic that he would, if he were logical, be forced to be agnostic about his own agnosticism and would not even be sure about the fundamental assumptions on which his uncertainty is based. We can score points this way—we can even reassure ourselves, but it is not likely that we will convince the agnostic; however, almost by definition, nothing is going to convince him. It's important that we convince ourselves that his half-way house is not, in fact, a half-way house between atheistic faith and theistic faith. Agnosticism in itself is yet another faith, another leap of the human intellect beyond that which it can conclusively demonstrate. By the very fact that he claims not to be able to solve the God question, the agnostic has come up with a solution—a solution which requires as much faith as do the other two solutions.

There are, as we mentioned in the last chapter, those who will contend that the agnostic position is a brave one—a refusal to seek solace from the mysteries of life through a belief in myths and fairy tales. Whether it is brave or merely stupid to say that the most basic kind

of question man can ask is unanswerable is not immediately obvious. It is true that a persuasive case could
be made that the man who does affirm meaning, purpose, and graciousness in reality has more faith than
he who shrugs his shoulders and refuses to face the
question. Indeed, a man of faith might be tempted to
say that the agnostic is, in fact, a theological Hamlet
who really can't make up his mind on the decisive
question because he is afraid to try.

It also should be observed in our dialogue, however
one-sided it may be with the agnostic, that even if his
solution may be satisfactory for himself and for his intellectual colleagues, it is not one that most of us who
live in the human condition are able to accept. It may
well be that the elite are able to struggle through life
without being able to answer with some kind of common sense its most basic question, but the vast majority of the human race need working assumptions. With
a shrug of his shoulders the agnostic will say, or imply,
that these are the unsophisticated, the superstitious, the
uninformed. Perhaps; but perhaps they are the merely
human who refuse to take seriously the notion that man
not only cannot fashion a serviceable answer to the
ultimate questions, but that he shouldn't even try.

In dialogue with the agnostics, the point is often
made that they are able to lead highly moral and dedicated lives without postulating the existence of a God—
that they have the highest kinds of professional and
personal standards, are faithful to their spouses, good
parents to their children, dedicated citizens of their

nation, without needing a God at all to guarantee such behavior. One must concede, and generously, that what they say is certainly true. Agnostics are, by and large, highly moral people; indeed, they tend on many occasions to be moralistic, and even puritanical; many of those I have worked with are better human beings than most Christians I know. I might go so far as to say that they are better Christians than many Christians I know.

What this proves is not immediately evident save that it does establish the fact that some people are able to lead highly moral lives without formally, at least, believing in God. I think that many of us poor, weak, and perhaps frequently immoral God-believers would be inclined to fall back on Gilbert Chesterton's poem about his friend Higgins, when we are faced with the stern, aloof, one might almost say puritanical, agnostic.

THE SONG OF THE STRANGE ASCETIC [1]

If I had been a Heathen,
    I'd have praised the purple vine,
My slaves would dig the vineyards,
    And I would drink the wine;
But Higgins is a Heathen,
    And his slaves grow lean and grey,
That he may drink some tepid milk
    Exactly twice a day

If I had been a Heathen,

[1] From *The Collected Poems of G. K. Chesterton* (New York: Dodd, Mead & Company, 1932), p. 199.

I'd have crowned Neaera's curls,
And filled my life with love affairs,
    My house with dancing girls;
But Higgins is a Heathen,
    And to lecture rooms is forced,
Where his aunts, who are not married,
    Demand to be divorced.

If I had been a Heathen,
    I'd have sent my armies forth,
And dragged behind my chariots
    The Chieftains of the North.
But Higgins is a Heathen,
    And he drives the dreary quill,
To lead the poor that funny cash
    That makes them poorer still.

If I had been a Heathen,
    I'd have piled my pyre on high,
And in a great red whirlwind
    Gone roaring to the sky.
But Higgins is a Heathen,
    And a richer man than I;
And they put him in an oven,
    Just as if he were a pie.

Now who that runs can read it,
    The riddle that I write,
Of why this poor old sinner,
    Should sin without delight—

But I, I cannot read it

(Although I run and run),
Of them that do not have the faith,
And will not have the fun.

It is to be feared that most of us human beings would be far more inclined to imitate the poet than to imitate Higgins. The fact that there are agnostics who can lead extraordinarily moral lives is impressive, but it does not follow that the vast majority of us are capable of doing this. However, the morality of agnostics is not the real point. Their lives establish that agnostics can be moral, but it does not establish that the agnostics are right.

I have worked closely with agnostics most of my life in the university environment, and the basic weakness of their position has nothing to do with their ethics but with the fact that they cannot cope with the critical question of the meaning of life and of the meaning of death. They are, for the most part, so paralyzed by the death phenomenon that they have refused to think or talk about it and do not know how to behave when death occurs in the family of one of their friends. If they could say that life is senseless and meaningless then they could be bitter and angry at the cruel universe of which they are a part; if they could say that life has purpose and rationale and can ultimately transcend itself, then they could face death with hope. But their agnostic position permits them neither alternative and therefore they must pretend as best they can that death does not exist or is not going to happen, or is not important.

Unfortunately, shallowness in the face of death means shallowness in the face of life, and agnosticism ultimately is a shallow and superficial response to the mystery of life. It may sustain an extraordinarily high level of morality, at least for a limited number of people, but it prevents the development of a dimension of depth which is necessary for a fully human life. The agnostic is committed to many things but he is not really sure that he can be committed fully to a life that he not only does not understand, but concerning which he rejects the possibility of understanding.

We have argued, therefore, in this chapter that the agnostic response, while apparently novel, is based on assumptions that are not new and involves an act of faith every bit as much as does theism and atheism. The agnostic may be a charming, highly moral man, but he cannot cope with the most profound realities of human existence and thus is not able to develop certain kinds of depth in his personality; his notions about human knowledge are limited, and his rejection of the possibility of answering the God hypothesis on the grounds that God cannot be empirically verified beg the question completely. Agnosticism is an attempt at a compromise between theism and atheism; although it is a popular attempt in academic circles, it cannot be called a terribly successful one and is not going to be a very permanent solution, since most men have always felt and probably always will feel that the question which the agnostic says cannot be answered, absolutely has to be answered.

the graciousness

of being

We have said before that the critical question man must ask himself is whether being is gracious. The word "gracious" is carefully chosen not merely because of its strict denotation, but also because of the many connotations it has. Thus, for example, when we speak of a "gracious" woman, we mean not merely one that is good and beautiful and charming, but one who somehow or other is able to communicate goodness and warmth and joy to those around her. The critical question man must ask is whether the reality in which he finds himself immersed has this same quality of graciousness as does the brilliant, charming, warm woman.

The phrase "graciousness of being" may at first sound strange to readers of this volume. It is a phrase that implies many things and it is difficult to narrow it to a strict definition. But what it implies basically is that life is good, not merely good in an abstract, theoretical way, but good in a hard, concrete, practical, happiness-producing way. It does not claim that life is

38

simply good, or unmitigatedly good (as we will note later on in the chapter, the "graciousness of being" is mixed with suffering and evil and misery), but to affirm the "graciousness of being" is to affirm, after careful consideration and investigation, one's basic faith that, even though the world is cursed with all kinds of evil, and even though there is much confusion and mystery about it, nevertheless it is still basically good rather than evil, beautiful rather than ugly, rational rather than chaotic, happiness-producing rather than tormenting.

The question, then, is whether reality is good; whether life is good; whether ultimately there is meaning, purpose, and beauty in the world; whether, in the final analysis, we can say the world is benign or whether we are forced to the conclusion that it is malign.

Man looks around him and sees before him beauty, goodness, and rationality in the world. He is not prepared to affirm immediately that the world itself is orderly, beautiful, good, and rational, since there are obviously many other qualities not so pleasant in the phenomena he observes. But he does see some signs of graciousness and he wonders if the graciousness he perceives is a deceit and an illusion. He observes that life has joy, happiness, laughter, challenge, and love, and he wonders if these are transient and deceptive realities; whether they are, in fact, a "phoniness" that hides the malignancy which is at the core of life and reality or whether the graciousness he perceives is rather a veil that partially hides not malignancy, but a much greater graciousness than he is yet able to comprehend. If we may thus rephrase the question, it is now to be stated as follows: Is the graciousness we perceive a monstrous illusion or a hint of something we do not yet perceive which is far better than we can imagine?

Since most of us probably would like to be optimists if we could be, the temptation to take the graciousness we perceive at its face value is very strong, but we are prevented from doing so by the problem of evil which inevitably and indeed automatically arises as soon as we have contemplated for but a brief period of time the phenomenon of graciousness, because while the world looks good, it also looks bad. It is filled with evil and suffering and death, with wars and race riots, with hatred, distrust, and fear, with misery and suffering, and with ignorance and poverty. If reality is gracious, and I rather like to think it is, then how can all these forms of ungraciousness be around? If the world is good, why is it filled with so much evil? Since man has begun to think, the problem of evil has been a major stumbling block to his profession of faith in graciousness—a stumbling block over which many have been unable to climb.

There is (and it might just as well be said honestly) not only no easy answer to the problem of evil, but there is really no answer at all. The evil is there, it will not go away, and try as we might we cannot give a satisfactory explanation as to how it could exist in a gracious universe. But it must be emphasized that he who solves the problem of evil by rejecting the graciousness of being and by concluding that the world is essentially evil has by no means solved all his problems, because if the world is evil, then how does one explain the phenomenon of graciousness? Why is the world not totally evil? The mixed nature of reality, partly good and partly evil, is a stumbling block either way, and just as the problem of evil is an obstacle to him who would profess faith in graciousness, so the problem of good is a gnawing doubt to him who would profess faith in malignancy. One is forced, in viewing the mixed nature of reality, to conclude that either evil or good is an illusion, but to so conclude requires a leap of faith, an act of belief despite at least some evidence to the contrary. Whether evil is illusion or good is illusion cannot be affirmed with confidence, save by the man who is willing to make an act of faith.

I have always thought that the solution to the two problems devised in ancient Persia was an ingenious and consoling one, though filled with logical and metaphysical inconsistencies. Those followers of Zoroaster rather cleverly concluded that the world, mixed bag that it was, had to be the result not of one transcendent reality but of two—one good and one evil; that the evil god and the good god contended with each other, and that the result of the contention was the confusion and the mess in which mankind lived. This was extremely useful as a short-run explanation of the problem with which we are dealing, though the weaknesses and the inconsistencies in it had never made it too popular.

Nonetheless, the temptation to see spirit as good and matter as evil has kept recurring down through the history of the human race, and if the followers of Zoroaster are not numerous in the world today, their Puritan intellectual descendants are still in abundance. Even the Zoroasterians finally had to make the leap one way or another; despite careful hedging, they were brave enough to concede that in the final analysis the good god was just a bit stronger than the evil one, and that he would triumph in the battle that was going on. Shrewd and hesitant as they were, the Zoroasterians ultimately made an act of faith in the graciousness of being. For faith in the graciousness of being means, in the final analysis, faith in the triumph of good over evil, and this is not an easy faith. If anything, it is a more difficult faith than the pessimistic faith which sees evil triumphing over good. That more men have chosen the former posture may indicate that more men are superstitious or weak, or simply that man is, for all his sufferings and miseries, still basically an optimistic animal.

In our day the contention between good and evil seems to have frequently resolved itself into the question of death partly because, while man is rapidly conquering most other physical evils and is making some progress toward conquering the moral evils, the bastions of death remain unweakened by his attacks. Secondly, Christianity has brought into sharp focus the whole question of the reality of death in a fashion that the previous world religions, to say nothing of the nature religions, were not so eager to attempt. The Christian quite bluntly says that death is the problem and that resurrection is the answer. Since the appearance of Christianity, Western culture has not been able to escape the question of resurrection and often finds itself forced to turn the question of the graciousness of being into the question of whether man does rise. This is an even more difficult question than the question of whether life is good.

Brian Wicker, a brilliant young English theologian, makes no bones about it. He says that the issue which humanism and Christianity must discuss is the issue of the resurrection, because in the commitment to the self-fulfillment of the human personality there is an implicit demand for resurrection; if death cuts short the fulfillment of the personality, then fulfillment is impossible and death frustrates and defeats the basic thrust and demand of the humanist mystique. Either man rises, according to Wicker, or humanism is every bit as much an illusion as Christianity, for a world without resurrection is an evil world; a world in which man does not rise is irrational; a world in which death triumphs is a world where men cannot be human. Can we believe, therefore, that death is strong enough to conquer the beauty and the goodness and the truth of the human spirit? Either response involves faith, and neither response is easy.

But someone who has been exposed to the Christian dialogue must at some point in the game ask himself whether an affirmation of the graciousness of being is also an affirmation of the fact of resurrection. It is not necessarily a question which must be faced immediately or explicitly. If the leap from skepticism to resurrection is too great, the more general question that still needs to be asked is, Is the world good—does life have meaning—is graciousness a myth? After all the agonies and the considerations, all the wrestlings and the torments, all the arguments and dialogues, the answer of the man of faith is—Damn it, yes, life is good, being is gracious, though at least in our experience of it the graciousness is mixed with evil. If our answer even then is still affirmative, we are forced to conclude that there is a God.

This is not to say that one deduces from the graciousness of being the fact that God exists. What is at issue is not a deduction but an explication. To say that being is gracious is the same thing as to affirm that God is, for God is merely the label we use to affirm the goodness, the rationality, the beauty of being. As some modern writers have clearly pointed out, the important question for man is not whether God exists, but whether He is *present* through and in the graciousness of being. If being is gracious, then God is present. The affirmation of the presence of God and the affirmation of the graciousness of being are the same. God is nothing more than the personification of the ultimate graciousness of reality. Man's decision as to whether life makes sense and whether it does have purpose and beauty and meaning and significance is the very same as the solution to the question of whether there is a God. We might go so far as to say that he who affirms the graciousness of reality affirms God, even though he may not realize it and even though he may implicitly deny God or shrug his shoulders in response to the God hypothesis. In this frame of reference it is altogether likely that a good many agnostics who, despite themselves, live as though reality is gracious, have in fact affirmed the God they do not know. The believer, of course, can perhaps a bit smugly console himself by the thought that the devout agnostic may not know God, but that God knows him, and that's all that really matters.

I am not at this point attempting to describe the nature of the graciousness that we affirm, or to sketch out precisely what it means to say that God personifies the order, beauty, and goodness in his ultimate triumph we have decided to believe. We certainly do not propose to identify God necessarily with the goodness, order, and beauty that we perceive in reality in the pantheistic sense. But I must remark in passing that if we believe, then we are ultimately forced to say that the principle of graciousness we witness in the world must ultimately transcend that which we perceive, though I would not venture to suggest how the transcendence occurs.

At this point, however, it is merely necessary to establish that the God issue and the issue of life and being are, in fact, the same issue. He who realizes that the affirmation of the graciousness of reality is the same thing as professing faith in God still has considerable problems to resolve as to what the nature of this God

is, whose presence he has perhaps unwittingly affirmed.
However, the fact that we have a hard time understanding the ultimate principle of graciousness (or, to
use Paul Tillich's words, the ground of being), and
that our language falls over itself trying to speak of
Him (or It, if you prefer), does not at all affect the
fact that we have affirmed that such a principle of graciousness is present. To put the matter more explicitly,
because we do not know who God is, and because we
find it terribly difficult to speak of Him, does not mean
that He is not, for any God that would be, necessarily
would be a God hard to know and almost impossible
to speak of. Even if we choose not to use the term
"God," and revert to speaking of the "Graciousness of
Being," we are still faced with the fact that the order,
rationality, beauty, goodness, and love we perceive in
the world are difficult to understand, and even more
difficult to speak of, and we are therefore forced to
fall back on the language of the poet, the philosopher,
and the lover. The measuring tape and the scale on
the cyclotron of the positivists are of little value in
speaking of either love or graciousness, and hence of
equally little value in speaking of God. But the dim-
ness of our understanding and the weakness of our
vocabulary does not lead us to believe that there is no
such thing as love or beauty; the fact that neither of
these can be programmed into a computer or repro-
duced in an experimental laboratory is hilariously ir-
relevant to him who is in love or has enjoyed beauty.
Similarly, once we have made the leap of faith into the

graciousness of being, we are hardly likely to be both-
ered by the fact that we cannot mathematically demonstrate that reality is indeed benign or that we cannot
refute with absolute conviction the problem of evil. We
are still disturbed by evil but we are so captivated by
good that we refuse to permit evil to distract our attention from good.

It is worth reasserting once again that either decision
which man makes in favor of benignity or malignancy
requires faith—requires a leap beyond the clearly de-
monstrable—beyond that which we can say on the
basis of overwhelming evidence. The atheist must believe every bit as much as the theist; he who rejects
resurrection has made an act of faith every bit as much
as he who accepts it. At first blush resurrection may
seem very unlikely, and yet it cannot be completely
excluded, either. Man must decide. Either decision is
an act of faith. No one can make a decision for him
and in a very real sense, no arguments can be advanced
for either side. No one can really convincingly persuade him, one way or another. As we shall suggest
in the final chapter, there is a way of knowing, but that
way comes after faith and not before it.

In this chapter we have asserted that belief in the
goodness and rationality of reality is, in effect, belief
in God's presence. God is the Ultimate Principle of the
Graciousness of Being. This assertion, this affirmation
of God's presence or the Graciousness of Being is not
easy or automatic because contrary evidence is power-
ful. The world is filled with good and evil and man

must decide which will triumph and which is an illusion. He who decides in favor of good decides for God; he who decides for irrationality and despair, however brave his syllogisms, has decided against God, against hope, and we are prepared to contend from the point of view of a believer, against that which is most noble in human aspirations.

God  talk

When the fiery French philosopher, Blaise Pascal, said that he wanted no part of the god of geometricians and mathematicians, but rather the God of Abraham and the God of Isaac and the God of Jacob, he was merely emphasizing very powerfully a perennial problem about God—the risks that our talk about Him will obscure the reality about which we are trying to talk far more than it will reveal it. Pascal's cry of anger is even more interesting when we stop to consider that he himself was one of the great mathematicians of all times.

But Pascal's point was well taken. God talk is difficult, but apparently necessary. Once man has decided that there is some ultimate principle of graciousness in reality, he simultaneously must talk about this principle and endure the frustrating realization that his talk has quite unsatisfactory tools for coping with the reality that he is trying to describe.

I have a young friend who is obsessed by God. There is little else in his conversation besides talk about God and the Church. But this young man belongs to no church and insists that he does not believe in God. He is a brilliant graduate student of philosophy—his major concern is the philosophy of religion and his specialty within that area is talk about God. The young man

49

insists that his philosophical research convinces him that one cannot talk about God; but it would appear, at least for the present time, that he intends to devote his professional career to a discussion of God talk, through which he will establish conclusively that one cannot talk about God. The irony, and even the humor, in his position has so far escaped him. He must talk about God and he must talk about God talk, and in the very act of doing so, he denies the possibility of exactly what he is doing. There are times when the ultimate principle of graciousness seems to behave almost like a hunting dog from which we cannot escape.

The young man's problem is not his alone, for the major trends in contemporary American philosophy are focused on the philosophy of language and the possibility of man discussing reality in any fashion. This question is an extraordinarily serious one that the philosophers have not yet satisfactorily resolved. It is not merely that on the philosophical level we cannot be confident when we speak about God; it is also that we cannot really be confident, at least in this philosophical tradition, when we speak about anything (my young man who can't stop talking about a God he can't talk about is forced to acknowledge that he can't talk about anything else either).

It is certainly not the purpose of this book to attack contemporary philosophy. Its concern about the significance of language is extraordinarily important, but when this concern is approached in such a fashion that the possibility of a solution is precluded and man cannot use language at all to speak about any kind of reality, then the outside observer is forced to comment that such a philosophical concern seems to have brought us to a blind alley. Man must speak about reality, even if his language is imprecise and inaccurate, and on occasion, deceptive. Similarly, man must speak about God; when the positive philosopher points out all the errors that he falls into in speaking about God and all the mistakes he makes, man (or at least most men) is not inclined to give up but simply redoubles his efforts to try and say something meaningful about the ultimate principle of graciousness. Our God talk may not be terribly adequate, but we are still going to keep talking.

It is often said, particularly by skeptics and unbelievers, that man creates God in his own image and likeness, which is an assertion that is certainly true, though it does not follow, as the unbelievers would like to persuade us, that therefore there is no Ultimate Principle of Graciousness. It merely follows that when man attempts to talk about graciousness he uses language that says something, however inadequate it may be, about God, and quite a bit, however terribly revealing it may be, about himself. Since man knows of no other reality that thinks and loves besides himself, he necessarily compares God to himself; he realizes, however dimly, that when he does this he runs the risk of leaving much unsaid about God that ought to be said. The point is that man has no choice but to describe God in cultural terms that are most familiar to him. That the ancient Hebrews conceived of Yahweh as rather like a fiery desert warrior chief does not mean Yahweh did not exist, but simply that for the children of Israel to speak of him required that they use a language equipped with categories that placed high values on the virtues and talents of the desert chieftain. Similarly, it was not at all surprising, indeed, on the contrary, it was inevitable, that later God talk would make the Ultimate Principle of Graciousness sound like a mathematician or a Father Abbott or a Great Hangman in the Sky, or a dull academician who was not even sure of his own existence, or a passionate lover, or an old, ill-tempered Irish monsignor.

The philosopher of language may be terribly upset by such language since it is not nearly precise enough to suit his requirements, but he must not forget that it is not scientific, but rather poetic language which is necessarily being used in God talk. God talk is poetry because poetry is the only tool that man really finds satisfactory when he tries to describe his relationships with the Ultimate Principle of Graciousness. If we think of God talk as poetry, then we are not surprised by its exaggerations and inadequacies. It still reveals to us something important even though we find it difficult to translate exactly what that important thing is in strict prose, and we are well aware that while the poet tells us something, and something indeed terribly important about the reality he is describing, he also tells us a great deal about himself.

The difficulties we have with God become clearer

when we tend to address ourselves to the question, "Is there a personal God?"—which is rephrased, generally, to mean, in effect, "Is the Ultimate Principle of Graciousness a person?" We immediately become bogged down on trying to define what a person is. It was clearly something different for the Fathers of the Councils of Ephesus and Chalcedon than it is for those who are familiar with the writings of Sigmund Freud. If by "person" we mean a reality associated with love and intelligence, there seems to be no real problem, since clearly the Graciousness of Reality involves goodness and order, love and rationality. But the word "person," as we are accustomed to use it, also implies limitation and imperfection. The "persons" we know are all finite like ourselves. Indeed "person" has come in our ordinary talk to mean roughly the equivalent of "human being," so that when we say "Is God a person?" we can also be saying "Is God a human being like us?" To that we must respond, even though some of the qualities and attitudes we attribute to God are really projections of our own qualities and attitudes, that God is not human as we are. Having said these things, we find ourselves thoroughly confused and wonder how we can get out of the dilemma of having to talk about a reality about which we cannot talk. Modern theologians are of some help to us when they say, in precise language, that we should affirm that it would be a mistake to deny that God possesses in some fashion the perfection that we imply when we use the word "person." Surely this is a precise and accurate enough statement, but it is not entirely satisfactory, and it leaves us wondering whether it is possible for us to communicate with the Ultimate Principle of Graciousness to, in Martin Buber's terms, enter into an I-Thou relationship with the Graciousness of Reality. Can we, in short, behave as though God were something like a person? The proper response seems to be—Why not? Even if we realize that the language we use in this behavior is poetic language, inadequate language, the human needs to commune with the Ultimate Principle of Graciousness are poetic needs. It is a tragic self-deception in this age of positivism to conclude that the poetic dimensions of the human personality are any less real or any less revealing than the scientific dimensions.

There are some modern theists, still affiliated with the Church and considering themselves religious people, who publish articles in which they insist that it is no longer necessary to pray. One man in particular is extremely interesting, because I have the impression from his writing that he refuses to pray partly because he feels that he does not need to and partly because he wants to punish God for having deceived us in the past about who He is. It is as if this writer were saying, "You are not the God I learned about in my catechism classes or in my theology courses, and therefore, O Principle and Graciousness, I'm not going to waste my time praying to You."

But surely this position is absurd. Man would need to pray even if there were not a God to pray to. The testimony of social science on this subject is conclusive. Men in every culture and of every age pray—not all men, but most men—and they pray because they need to pray. They pray to affirm their relationship with the goodness and graciousness of the universe (though perhaps in some instances it is also to placate the malign powers that are abroad in the world), to reassure themselves of the basic bonds of unity which unite them to the forces of the natural world, to ratify once again the bonds of unity that hold them to their fellow men, and finally, to assert the basic unity of man with himself. Prayer is communion with nature, with goodness, with one's fellow men, and with one's own personality, and he who refuses to pray finds a great and empty vacuum in his life. In the words of the distinguished sociologist, Everett C. Hughes: [1]

> Those who have the cure of souls in their charge —pastors, psychiatrists—can tell better than I what burdens break and what sicknesses ravage the souls of those who, in the name of self-reliance, emancipation or progress, try to act as if there were no cycle of youth, maturity, old age, and death; no rhythms of inner peace and conflict, of guilt and freedom from guilt, of grief and of the healing of its wounds. . . .
>
> How ghastly can be the smile of a suffering man who is pretending that all is well; how pathetic the stiff but tottering stance of a man who, because he

[1] Everett C. Hughes, *Men and Their Work* (Chicago: University of Chicago Press, 1959), pp. 17 and 18.

does not know how to share his troubles with others through the historic liturgies, is about to break under them. How pathetic, also, the man who, in his time of trouble, expresses the ultimate of that individualism in which we have all been reared—the insistence that his troubles are so private and so unique that no social salve can soothe them.

The universality of this human need for prayer could even be used, though I shall not attempt to use it so, as an argument that there is a God, since the universal hunger for absolute goodness and absolute love could hardly come to be unless there was a reality to which it corresponded. But even if one does not wish to use this argument before the affirmation of the Graciousness of Being, once one has concluded that there is a principle of graciousness in reality, we are almost forced to say that graciousness would not be very gracious if it produced in man the need for prayer when there was nothing which could respond to such communication.

We then must ask ourselves whether God needs prayer, and the answer to that should not be so very difficult. Yahweh made it perfectly clear in the Old Testament that the sacrifices and the holocausts of the children of Israel were not particularly important to Him, but still man has considered prayer so important that he has often spoken of God in such a way that it would seem that God is angry or offended or hurt if man does not pray to Him. This must be understood once again as poetry, designed to convey the necessity flowing from the depths of human nature for prayer.

But there is another sense in which it can be said that God does need human prayer, and from this point we can make some extremely interesting and useful conclusions. Increasingly, men are persuaded that not only is reality gracious, but that graciousness is evolving. Since Charles Darwin, it has been clear that the world in which we live is an evolutionary world. The brilliant French paleontologist, Teilhard de Chardin, describes this as an evolution toward the fulfillment of graciousness. Graciousness is not static and stable. It is, rather, a growing, developing, evolving reality and the Ultimate Principle of Graciousness is not merely an alpha which sets the forces of graciousness to work but also an omega toward which graciousness is moving in its process of self-fulfillment. To put the matter a bit more specifically, God is not only the origin of evolution, but also the goal.

Teilhard sees the processes of evolution developing down through the ages toward the emergence of man, a being with the power of knowledge and love, and asserts the existence of a Noosphere, that is to say the bonds of unity and love which unite man to his fellow men and which now gird the world as do the physical and biological spheres. The Noosphere, that is to say, the Appearance of Man, is a major breakthrough in the evolutionary process. Man's struggle for more perfect knowledge, more satisfying love, is the summit of the evolutionary process.

There is not only beauty but plausibility in Teilhard's theorizing. Man's commitment to the search for truth and the quest for love represents not merely the most noble activity the world has ever seen, but also an ever-advancing movement of the evolutionary process of graciousness seeking to become completely gracious. If we are then asked one of the most critical questions modern man can ask about any reality, "Is God relevant?", we will respond, "Yes, indeed." He is not only relevant as the fountain and the source of graciousness, but He is even more relevant as the goal toward which reality is evolving, as that omega toward which our struggle in the growth of graciousness is aimed; our efforts to overcome evil, suffering, ignorance, worry, misery, distrust, and eventually even death, are part of the evolution of graciousness, and are by no means without purpose. Is God relevant? Of course He is relevant, because as the omega point He is the aim of all gracious activity—not merely the aim, but also the goal, the warmth, the charm of goodness which attracts all toward it. As Augustine said it in much less complicated language, "Thou hast made us for Thyself alone, O Lord, and O Lord our hearts are restless 'till they rest in Thee." When Charles Peguy told us that man was the pilgrim of the absolute, he was not being merely rhetorical. Man is on pilgrimage, and his own efforts are part of a vast process of pilgrimage, for it is the fulfillment of graciousness.

Now having established, at least as a working hypothesis, the Teilhardist scheme, we return to the question of whether God needs our prayers or whether He needs our efforts at all. One brilliant young modern theologian has suggested to me an extremely useful way of thinking about God in this context, and that is to speak of Him as the Master Improvisor, as the great expert at "playing it by ear." The principle of graciousness has a goal and a plan, a plan that will be fulfilled, but a plan which also needs our cooperation for its fulfillment, and God, much as though He were a dancer or a jazz musician, adjusts His motions, His activities, His responses to our motions, activities, and responses. Life is a dance or a jazz concert, with God improvising in response to what we do and how we develop and how we commit ourselves to the question of goodness and truth and beauty. We cannot frustrate His plan, and yet we are necessary for its fulfillment.

It should be observed, of course, that, like all other God talk, the last paragraph is highly poetic, but at least it is consciously so. It does not resolve the probably insoluble question of the relationship between Divine Power and human freedom, but it does suggest that God needs us and that the ultimate principle of graciousness cannot fulfill itself in the reality in which we are immersed without our help. We need graciousness, but It (or He, if you wish) needs us. God is indeed relevant to us, even though it is hard to talk about Him, but we are relevant to Him, and perhaps He finds it considerably less difficult to talk about us.

growing up religious

So far we have discussed man's decision on the critical question of graciousness as though it were made in splendid isolation, as though each individual, quite independent of his social-cultural background and his psychological history, decides for himself whether reality is gracious or not. But this is not the nature of the human condition. A person's cultural background, his social class, and his childhood experiences shape the context of his decision and have a profound influence on the nature of that decision. This is not to argue that man is not free to decide. In the final analysis, most men do have the capacity to choose between alternatives. But the nature, depth, and direction of this choice is always in a context, and the context is created by the past—the past of his family, his ethnic group, his culture, and, indeed, the past of the whole human race.

In this chapter we wish to say something about the psychological and sociological factors that can impinge on the decision for or against graciousness, because only when a person is able to understand something of his own background, and something of the context in which he lives and works and decides, will he be able to sort out the true questions from the false questions and the phony issues from the real issues.

Faith, at least the sort of faith that we are discussing in this volume, is rooted in trust. It would be a lot easier for a man who has learned to trust his fellow men and to trust the world in which he lives to decide that reality is gracious, than it would be for one whose personality-shaping experiences incline him to suspicion and distrust. In discussing this complex subject, we lean very heavily on the work of Charles William Stewart, in his book, *Adolescent Religion*.[1] Stewart very ingeniously uses the psychological framework of Erik Erikson to discuss the problem of growing up religious. He says:

> There are precursors of faith and attitudes and modes in the child's developmental history. However these undergo a transformation and enlargement or a radical transmutation as they are related to ultimate reality (God), particularly in early adolescence as the objects of faith are depersonalized and defamilyized and as the reality of the Wholly Other becomes apparent to the youth.[2]

Stewart finds four roots of faith in the early experiences of life. The first is to be found in the preverbal sense of security or trust which the infant feels with his mother. He experiences this through responding to his mother's empathy and physiologically by being

[1] Charles William Stewart, *Adolescent Religion* (Nashville, Tenn: Abingdon Press, 1967).
[2] *Ibid*, p. 253.

nursed, having his hunger satisfied, and by contact with his mother's body. He needs this trust basically as he needs food. If the earliest sensations of a child are not such as to create some sense of reassurance, it will be very difficult for the child, later on, to trust anyone or to make an act of faith in the goodness of reality. One advisedly says "very difficult"; if the earliest childhood experiences are distinctly unpleasant it does not become impossible for someone to experience trust, but he will do so only at the price of considerable effort and suffering.

According to Stewart, the second root of faith is in the "autonomy" drive which the child experiences, say from the age of two on. We all know children who are called "terrible twos." Until this age the infant is generally placid and docile and quite dependent, but as he becomes confident of his ability to walk, to provide for himself in some fashion, and to shape his own thoughts into words, he becomes very rambunctious and embarks upon a period of rebelliousness which may last for several months or even several years. What is happening is that the infant is discovering a sense of himself over against his parents, particularly when his parents oppose the things he wants. He is quite anxious about being separated from his parents. He also now is conscious of his own wants and desires, his own needs and independence. This first rebellion is the most courageous thing that any of us ever do and also the most risky. Without it we cannot really develop a sense of ourselves. If our parents sustain us in this rebellion, encourage us to be free, while at the same time laying down boundaries beyond which our rebellion cannot go and limits beyond which we cannot exercise our freedom, we grow into a more sophisticated understanding of reality and discover that we can, indeed, be ourselves but we cannot have or be everything. We develop both a feeling of freedom and a sense of the limitations of the possible. The child who successfully survives the autonomy crisis is neither overdependent on reality nor in total rebellion against it, and hence, with his relative freedom, is able at a later stage in life to critically evaluate his potentiality for graciousness.

On the other hand, if he is not able to move satisfactorily through the autonomy crisis, he will acquire feelings of guilt and shame for his rebellion, but still feel profoundly the need to rebel. The combination of rebellion and guilt and shame will harass him for the rest of his life and will prejudice him against faith in the graciousness of reality.

The third root of faith occurs in the years from four to six when the child is engaged in the process of sexual identification. He is now fully aware that one parent is of the same sex as he and the other parent of a different sex, and that the parent of the opposite sex seems more in love with the other parent than with the child. In this subtle interaction triad of mother, father, and child, the child must resist the temptation to reject his own sexuality and to identify with the parent who is of the opposite sex. In the process he must convert his animosity toward the parent of the same sex into an identification with that parent, and thus make possible a healthy relationship with the parent of the opposite sex. The process is complicated, and one need not be overly Freudian in one's explanation of it to see how important it is in a child's development of a sense of confidence in his own being. A boy who has profound doubts, misgivings, and uncertainty about his own masculinity, and a girl who deeply resents the fact that she is a girl, are not likely to be well disposed toward reality which, in making them sexual, has played a dirty trick on them. Identification with the parent of the same sex, instead of rivalry toward that parent, inclines the child to the suspicion that reality might, indeed, be gracious. Identification with the parent of the opposite sex and rejection of the parent of the same sex so befuddles and confuses the child that he feels very uncertain and ambiguous about the whole of the world in which he finds himself immersed.

The fourth and last root of faith is to be found in the so-called latency years from six to twelve when a young person to some extent leaves home and family behind to enter school and close relationship with his peer group. He discovers that his group, friends, and playmates are not nearly as favorably disposed toward him as were his family and that he has to win support and approval from this group or find himself rejected by it. It therefore becomes necessary that in some fashion the young person learn to conform—that is, to harmonize his needs, roles, and activities with those of others of his own age. If, on the basis of his past experience, he is reasonably secure and confident in his own selfhood, he can go along with the needs of the community without losing himself through total conformity. He can, in other words, learn to cooperate and still remain autonomous. But if he is not strong enough to contend with this new challenge, he either isolates himself from the community or surrenders himself completely to it. His "conformity crisis" is not successfully mastered, and the beginnings of alienation from his fellows have been made. He, then, who is able to integrate himself harmoniously with others without losing himself, has some confidence in the goodness of his membership in the human race and reason to think that reality might be gracious. But he who is either isolated or a total conformist is inclined to agree with the French philosopher that Hell is other people, and find himself extremely skeptical about the graciousness of being.

The next crisis, and one with which most young people today are most familiar, is the crisis of adolescence, the so-called identity crisis—the time when a person discovers who he is and in what he believes. As Erikson points out repeatedly, identity cannot come without ideology. One must have an ultimate loyalty—some person, cause, or cosmic whole to which to commit himself. In Erikson's terminology, this is the virtue of fidelity which enables one to devote oneself to something or someone as true. In the crisis of identity, the young person is challenged . . . discovering not just who he is, but to what he will commit himself. The previous religious training he has received provides him with the data—symbols, rituals, and theology—with which to ponder the problem. His prior emotional history has further given him the experience of trust or distrust, risk or rebellion, conformity or non-conformity that he will bring into this critical period.

If we agree with Erikson's and Stewart's analysis, we are forced to conclude that the crisis of faith in adolescence and the crisis of identity are the same thing; the young person's determination of the nature of reality is essential to his determination of the nature of himself. The way has been prepared for it by his past experiences, and the success with which he has mastered the crisis of trust, the crisis of autonomy, the crisis of identification, and the crisis of conformity will either facilitate or hinder his behavior in the crisis of ideology and identity. It therefore follows that he who finds himself inclined to one decision or another about the graciousness of being must understand himself and his own past to see whether his decision is based on a real understanding of the issues or merely on projections and frustrations from his past.

We should say a word about the next crisis that Erikson describes. He calls it the "crisis of intimacy"; in it the young person, now at the very end of adolescence (in the college years, perhaps), must decide whether he can give and receive in love, whether he is worth loving and capable of offering love. It does not seem to be much of an exaggeration to say that he who is not able to profess belief in the goodness of reality and the graciousness of being would be extraordinarily hesitant to give and receive love, because the intimate union between two lovers is bound to be deceptive and destructive if reality is not gracious.

Stewart sees five possible outcomes in the crisis of faith and the crisis of adolescent identity. Two of them are pathological. The young person may fixate at a previous crisis point and become either an isolate (and occasionally a psychotic isolate) or a rebellious delinquent, in both instances quite completely at odds with reality and with his fellow men. He also may refuse to make a decision and be content with conformity—in one type of conformity identifying with the church and religion and accepting the traditional ideology and values of parents and church without ever having seriously investigated. Or he may reject these values without seriously considering them and conform to the values of the world, or that part of the world in which he finds himself.

Finally, he may become autonomous, deciding for himself some sort of religious commitment, and commit himself freely to a set of values that are able to sustain life.

In our frame of reference the last group could include men who are committed to the graciousness of being, and also could, we suspect, include men who are not, but in both instances, since autonomy is postulated, we are presuming that we are dealing with people who have seriously and rigorously faced the question of the graciousness of being and have not copped out short of a decision.

If the analysis we are pursuing is correct, then it follows that the crisis of faith might be more appropriately entitled the crisis of religious identity or the crisis of religious maturity. Until the adolescent period, the child's religion is the religion of his parents, teachers, and clergy. His faith in the graciousness of being is a child's faith. He believes that being is gracious because he is told it is gracious. Now he must make his own choice; he does not accept the goodness of the world because people tell him it is good, but rather because he has taken a cold, hard look at it and decided for himself that it is good—or at least more good than evil; the crisis of religious maturation is the crisis whereby the faith of the child becomes the faith of the adult; unfortunately it is often complicated by the fact that, even though parents and teachers and clergy may tell a child that reality is gracious, from the child's viewpoint the reality that his adults present to him does not seem gracious and it does not even seem that the adults themselves act as though it were gracious.

There may have been a time in the history of the human race when the adolescent religious transition was a relatively easy one, when everything in the familial and cultural experience of a child made it very easy for him to accept parental religious values through adolescence into adulthood and then to reaffirm them as his own adult values without any great deal of anxiety and difficulty. But this was true only when the world was such that there was but one religious ideology available in the marketplace of ideas. One either accepted the graciousness of being or one did not. Most people did and then believed what their parents had believed before them, or at least honored the Gods that their parents had honored before them. But in our day the marketplace of ideologies is rich in abundance, whether one decides that being is gracious or not. Indeed, the decision itself is made more difficult because the issues that are at stake are obscured by the very richness of the offerings that the marketplace provides. The adolescent is a consumer, not only in clothes and phonograph records, but also in religious ideas and ideologies; there is a vast number of wares available for him to choose from and while this very vastness makes the choice more interesting and its results more challenging, it also necessarily implies struggle and pain.

However, the struggle and pain of the crisis of religious ideology is an inevitable price of freedom. It is a necessary prerequisite to authentic and mature religiousness. There is still enough of the traditionalist past with us that it is possible for someone to decide in favor of traditional religion. It can be mediocre, but one suspects that this will be less true in years to come. The marketplace and religious ideas may grow richer, but the products being marketed and the differences between them will become clearer. One will know that one cannot be religious without choosing the graciousness of being and acting as though one's life and ethics are essential for the self-fulfillment of graciousness. If one wishes to be religious then one must be religious. If one decides that being is gracious, then one must act as though it were gracious. But he who does not wish to do this can satisfy himself with some other ideology that makes life possible, or at least bearable. It does not impose the demands that a clear-cut solution in favor of graciousness would impose. But one suspects that eventually even this sort of escape will not be possible; that from that time there will be great clarity of issues. Men will either choose for the graciousness of being and behave according to their faith, or utterly reject it and behave in strict accordance with their rejection. However, this day is not yet, and it is still possible to get "hung up" on our pilgrimage of the absolute.

detours on the pilgrimage of the absolute

In the last chapter we suggested that man's decision for or against the graciousness of being is part of his religious maturation process and that his childhood experience, as well as his social class and culture, have profound influence on the way he makes his decision. It would follow that the various emotional and psychological fixations which may emerge during the developmental process can impede one's decision about the nature of reality and even so cloud the issues that the decision may be aborted. Under such circumstances, a person may move into chronological adulthood and maintain adolescent religious attitudes, which is to say, attitudes that decide, for superficial and childish reasons, either for or against the graciousness of being.

Ideally, the crisis of faith, or the crisis of religious identity, or the crisis of religious maturation—call it what we will—ought to be an experience of growth and development. One should seriously examine the claims of graciousness, God, faith, and religion, and weigh the pros and cons at some considerable length; even though such predominantly intellectual considerations do not substitute for the leap of faith (be it an atheistic or theistic faith), they will at least clarify the issues and clear away the misunderstandings and the imprecisions that obscure exactly what kind of leap is involved in an act of faith.

Furthermore, the young person should especially engage in a profound and realistic examination of his own religious tradition to determine whether he can live with the tradition. It is not merely intellectual honesty that indicates such an examination of one's own tradition, but also psychological wisdom. Whether we like it or not, the religious tradition of our family provides the religious atmosphere in which we were raised, even if it was not a particularly devout religious atmosphere. This tradition, then, is very much a part of us and of our orientation toward the world around us. It has made a deep impression on us and we cannot give it up lightly or cavalierly because it will remain to haunt us. He who attempts to run away from his own religious tradition without a fight, so to speak, is exposing himself to the risk of serious emotional strain as the years go on. Something that is as much a part of him as his religious tradition can only be rejected explicitly after acquiring a deep conviction based on extremely careful examination, that such a tradition is unsuitable, not geared to the best of one's needs, and to the demands of reality. If one is going to alienate oneself from one's past, one had better be certain that one understands precisely why one is doing it and have an alternative ideology to replace the one that is being rejected. The faiths of our youths are not easily cast aside.

But this careful examination both of the question of the graciousness of being and of the question of one's own religious tradition frequently does not happen. The young person drifts away from religion for no particularly good reason and then, as years go on, drifts back, again for no particularly good reason. The departure from religion, whether it be gradual or abrupt, is frequently part of the revolt against the adult world which is characteristic of the teen years. But for the adolescent to be dissatisfied with the adult world is not necessarily a bad idea, particularly if his dissatisfaction and revolt is selective. Unselective and total revolt is likely to be an emotional binge with little or no hard-headed and intelligent criticism of precisely those elements of the adult world which the young person does not like. Such total revolt is almost always followed in a few years by total compromise in which the young person makes his peace with the established disorder and accepts precisely those values of his parents against which he most strongly revolted.

It might be added that he, himself, will be just as puzzled by his children's blind revolt as his parents were by his. At no point in this adolescent outburst against his progenitors is there much in the way of serious and critical thought about what values from the traditional culture can be accepted and what the young person should reject; hence total rejection generates, a few years later, total acceptance.

The church, and through the church, religion, and through religion, God, are identified with parental society. It might be remarked that usually this identification is not entirely unjustified, since it is so very easy for the churches to become the chaplains of the established order and devote most of their time and concern to legitimating the values that the young person perceives in his parents. Furthermore, the religious functionaries of the churches are adults themselves who are identified with the values of other adults and represent almost in caricature precisely what the young person thinks is wrong with his parents and their philosophy of life.

Such situations may be even worse when the young person's past relationships with his parents turn the adolescent revolt from a normal and healthy part of developmental process into a neurotic rebellion. The church becomes identified with mother and God with father; since the young person feels guilty about being explicit even in his own mind about his hatred for his parents, he turns God and the church into scapegoats for the frustration and unhappiness in his life.

The church perhaps must bear some share of the blame for the scapegoat role in which it is cast, because frequently churchmen act in such a way as to make them almost ideal scapegoats (on occasion the church can even become a scapegoat for the animosity a young person feels toward a spouse in a marriage that is not working out). But the rejection of God and religion and the church because some churchmen act in such a way that a young person can think of God and the church as mother and father has nothing to do with the basic decision on whether being is gracious; if we can view these identifications from some sort of distant perspective, we are forced to say that it is a strange, weird fate for ultimate graciousness to be rejected precisely because it has become confused in a young person's mind with unhappy parental relationships, relationships which in young people's experience represent the perversion of graciousness.

To put the matter more bluntly, the revolt against God, religion, and the church is, in many if not most cases, a revolt against one's family; the revolt is based on almost no investigation of the intellectual foundations of the claims of religion and no even remotely objective consideration of the basic issue of the graciousness of reality. To revolt is almost an end in itself and is anything but an occasion for careful and serious consideration of the meaning of life. The youthful rebel, as a matter of fact, wants no part of any such consideration, because to face sensibly and realistically the claims of graciousness would be to deprive him of the marvelous relief for his aggressions that religious revolt provides. Unfortunately, such a revolt is self-defeating. It contributes nothing to emotional or religious maturity and, in fact, since it is a fixation, inhibits both processes. The brave adolescent religious rebel who thinks he is striking out for freedom is in many instances the prisoner of his own frustrations, neuroses, and unexpressed animosities. He is not addressing himself to the basic religious questions and probably never will. The period of revolt will come to an end, at least in most cases, and will be replaced by the same sort of childish religious attitudes he had before the revolt and which, at one period in his life, he claimed to have despised in his parents. The question of the graciousness of reality is never faced in an adult fashion. For a few years or a few months he was a rebel without a cause, and now he is no longer a rebel and has neither a cause nor an identity. His rebellion, indeed, was a form of massive self-deception.

But we cannot simply leave the matter here. Young people are very dissatisfied with their churches; in many instances the churches stand in the way of God and in the way of adult decisions about graciousness. This problem of young people and their churches has to be investigated in more detail, not merely because if a decision is made for graciousness, then presumably the young person must set about renewing and reforming his church, but also because, unless he comes to an understanding of what there is in the church that disturbs him, the young person may well use the weakness of his church as a pretext for not facing the much more difficult question of graciousness.

There are four needs that contemporary young people experience very powerfully that religion ought to respond to but for which, in most instances, it seems to fail to provide the proper response.

First of all the young person wants meaning, but he has learned to be skeptical of all systematic explanations. As he grows up he sees the confusion and uncertainty that abound in the world around him—war, racial unrest, automation, the mechanization of life, destruction of natural resources—but he has strong doubts about his ability to understand the meaning of these troubles, much less to provide an answer for them. The public sphere of life—that is to say, life beyond intimate friendships and family relationships—seems to be a place where coherent theories and explanatory propositions are not to be found. In the public sector of one's life, one must be skillful, aggressive, and diligent, but one cannot expect coherence, satisfaction, or friendship, and one therefore is inclined to withdraw one's emotional commitments from this sector and seek satisfaction in the private sector of life; but one has an uneasy feeling that even here the chaos of the world outside will ultimately penetrate.

The young person wants meaning, needs meaning, but cannot find it. The official meaning-giving institutions, and particularly the universities, seem to have despaired of finding any explanation for life and respond to the young person's questions with an agnostic shrug. Religious institutions repeat the pieties of the past, but in a language and style that lead the young person to suspect that there is no substantive content in these pieties. He therefore looks at the various meaning-providing institutions and says, "You and your ideologies are responsible for the mess the world is in. Why should I take you seriously? Why should I even expect to find a coherent and systematic explanation of the phenomena I experience?" This skepticism about ideology extends even to the various leftist and Marx-

ist ideologies that satisfied the youth a generation ago
and most of the young people in the New Left are pas-
sionately anti-ideological. They want "love" to be the
only ideology that is necessary. The hippies push this
anti-ideological inclination to its ultimate extreme when
they reject anything but love as a value in life, a rejection which, of course, makes love itself impossible.

*Secondly, the young person wants to "belong," but is
skeptical of organizations.* Ever since Western man de-
serted the peasant villages for the industrial metropolis,
he has sought to reestablish some of the intimacy, the
warmth, the social support of the peasant community.
But modern man, particularly in his youthful variety,
has made this quest for community a highly conscious
and explicit search. He wants deep, intimate, and
meaningful relationships; he wants to belong to something that is important, but he is extremely skeptical of
any organized attempt to create such a community and
the battle cry, "Not another organization," echoes and
reechoes on the college campus.

Such a reaction is not surprising. The young person
looks around him; he sees that most organizations are
big, not to say gigantic; big business, big labor, big
government, big education, big church. In none of these
does there seem to be room for himself and for the
development of the uniqueness of his own personality.
In his judgment the giant organization exists to snuff
out the creativity of the human spirit, and to crush the
uniqueness of the human person. If he is told that organizations exist to promote community and not to

repress it, to create a climate in which the human spirit can flower instead of destroying it, he will skeptically respond that this may be so, but it is not true of most of the organizations he knows, including his church. The young person, therefore, wants meaning and belonging—meaningful belonging and belonging which bestows meaning. Presumably it is precisely these two needs that the churches are designed to satisfy, and yet, even though many churchmen may be afraid to admit it, most young people do not find these needs met in most of the ecclesiastical institutions that now exist. If the churches are such feeble failures in that which they are supposed to do best, the young person may perhaps be forgiven for at least having some initial doubts about whether the church's message about God and the graciousness of being ought to be accepted at face value. Indeed, on occasion, one suspects that the young person will make his act of faith, his commitments to God and to graciousness, not because of his church but despite it.

Thirdly, the young person seeks challenge and the opportunity for service. Perhaps no other generation in the history of the human race has been as enthusiastically committed to unselfish service of its fellow men than has the present generation of young Americans. It is not always the consistent or reliable or even very mature variety of generosity, but generosity it is. *However, the need for service must be reconciled with the fear of corruption in idealism if one becomes too heavily engaged in service.* It does not take the young person long to realize that love by itself is not enough and that the suffering and misery in the world is likely to be un- dented by simple unskilled and untrained love. If he wishes really to effect change in society, the young per- son will have to acquire skills and competencies. He will have to make a life-long commitment to such ser- vice, a commitment that inevitably will involve him in the dirty, messy world of practical affairs, a world where he may have to be satisfied with progress that is less than perfect, with solutions that are less than com- plete, and with courses of action which appear danger- ously like compromise.

Rather than have his ideals tainted by such corrup- tion, the youthful altruist may very well abandon his attempt at service and live in a world where his ideals are very high, but where they have no impact on life around him (which may be saying that he will end up as a college teacher). Here, too, the churches have been less than successful. They have not been able to offer young people the kind of opportunities for service that are challenging and the ethical vision that will en- able them to make further commitments to a world which is less than perfect, and which will be only some- what improved by their efforts. The church is not able to offer much in the way of reasons for faith that one does not labor in vain.

Finally, perhaps the most serious dilemma the young person faces is that he wants desperately to love—to give himself in love—but he is not sure that he is worth loving. Raised in a highly competitive society and trained from the very beginning in the techniques for success in this society, the young person frequently does not experience enough unconditioned love to have faith in his own value or goodness. He learns quickly that he is loved when he performs well, when he succeeds, when he produces the kind of behavior his parents expect. But if he fails, if he does not produce and conform, then love is withdrawn. If this is the only kind of love he experiences, then he will never learn to accept trust and to love himself. He must, as he matures, periodically experience a love which says to him, "I love you when you are good, I love you when you are bad. When you are bad I sometimes must punish you but I do so always in the context of my love for you. I love you when you succeed, I love you when you fail. I love you when you perform well and I love you when you make a fool out of yourself. I love you not because of what you can do, but I love you because of who you are, and I shall always love you." The self-suspicion, self-distrust, self-rejection, self-hatred, and self-punishment which plague the lives of so many young Americans are the result of this conditioned love, and what young people need in their adolescent and college years is reassurance; they need to be told that they are good, they are valuable, they are worth something, that their life will amount to something, that they are capable of doing good and great things. It need not be pointed out in any great detail that most ecclesiastical organizations have been notably unsuccessful in whatever attempts they have made to manifest such reassurance and love.

From the young person's point of view, then, there are reasons for considerable skepticism about organized religion, but he must be wary of identifying the failure of the churches with the failure of graciousness, and equally wary of concluding that because his church has failed him, it follows that his religious tradition has failed him. He must first discover whether there is a plausibility in the graciousness of being, and then whether there are elements in his religious tradition that respond to his needs for meaning, belonging, challenge, and love. If there are, then he should seek out such elements both because they do represent that which is good and true and because they are probably the most likely place where he can find satisfaction for his human needs.

The young person, therefore, who is striving for an answer to the God question must not become distracted from the basic issues either by rebellion against parental society or by massive dissatisfaction with the ecclesiastical organizations. Both these institutions may need reform and renewal, but their failures and inadequacies have nothing to do, necessarily, with one's decision on whether being is gracious; to permit rebellion or dissatisfaction to impede his decision is an immature escape.

 **alternates to God**

In an earlier chapter we spoke of the three logical approaches to the question of God: the theistic one which affirms that there is a God, the atheistic one which denies it, and the agnostic response which refuses either to affirm or deny that there is a God. We also argued that, when the question is rephrased to the Graciousness of Reality, the agnostic compromise does not seem to be logically valid. However, when we began to consider the psychological, social, and cultural context in which man makes a decision on the God issue, we realized that there is a whole marketplace of ideologies from which the contemporary young person shops much as he does for consumer goods, and that psychologically and socially there are a number of compromises, accommodations and escapes by which the young person can avoid basic issues in the God question or resolve the problem in a superficial fashion which releases him from any obligation for taking the implications of his decision very seriously. The ancient compromise of choosing to believe in God in theory but running one's practical life according to other values has not lost its popularity. Even though we expressed the conviction that the possibility of such escapes and compromises would decline in years to come, we are still forced to acknowledge that at the present time the open market of ideology is cluttered with seemingly attractive products. We must therefore investigate some of these products if only so that the young person may not be able to deceive himself as to what the root question really is.

There are, first of all, those who reject God but affirm graciousness, the devout and virtuous agnostics of whom we previously talked. This reaction to the God question is not, in fact, a denial of God or of graciousness. What the devout agnostic rejects is really a phony, out-of-date, inadequate notion of God, a notion which he does well to reject, although the weak link in his armor is his inability to realize that there are other notions of God which cannot be put aside so readily. The devout agnostic is caught on the horns of a dilemma and it is only by obscuring the issues that he is able to affirm graciousness and shrug his shoulders at the question of transcendence and resurrection. The devout agnostic grows silent in the face of death; his faith in graciousness is unable to cope with this absolute event.

There are also those, and they are a much larger group, who affirm God but, at least by implication, deny graciousness, and the scriptures are not particularly gentle with this sort of person. Jesus told the parable of the two sons, one of whom said to the father that he would do what he commanded but in fact did not do it, and the other who said, "I will not," but in fact went and did what was commanded. It was the second son who found favor in the father's eyes. Again Jesus remarked that not everyone who says "Lord,

Lord," shall enter the Kingdom of Heaven, and finally, he chose to address the most "religious" men of his time as a brood of vipers and described them as whitened sepulchers all shiny on the outside and filled with dead men's bones on the inside. The mere affirmation of God is clearly not enough if it does not carry with it conviction about graciousness in action according to this conviction.

Those who affirm God and deny graciousness are not merely those who have some sort of nominal belief in God and church affiliation, but lead what has traditionally been called sinful lives. They also include those who are avowedly pious and devout but whose religious views are narrow, cramped, bigoted, oppressive, and gloomy, despite impressive external displays of piety. Some of them may be pillars of the church. Indeed not everyone who says "Lord, Lord" shall enter into the Kingdom of Heaven, because not everyone who says "Lord, Lord" really believes in the Graciousness of Reality and not everyone who says "Lord, Lord" escapes the temptation to turn the personification and the symbol of graciousness into a God of malignancy.

Yet another substitute for religion is to be found in the new "religions" which crowd into the marketplace of ideas. The religion of science, the religion of freedom, the religion of revolution, the religion of psychoanalysis, the religion of black power, the religion of service of "the people." These are new mythologies which can serve as outlets for human idealism and generosity as well as an escape from a conscious and explicit decision about graciousness. There are also men and women who turn their careers, their family life, the pursuit of money, of power, of "fun" into virtually a religion, since in the absence of an explicit decision about the God question, these means can become ends in themselves, ends which are consuming and distracting but ultimately not very satisfying.

Behind all these escapes there is almost inevitably an implicit decision about graciousness and perhaps even an explicitly phrased decision about God, though at least for most of the men and women committed to these substitute religions there has not been a carefully thought out and explicit decision about graciousness. In many instances the substitute religion, however attractive and persuasive it may be, and however true it may be up to a point, is a conscious substitute for an even more basic question than the God question, at least as those who profess the new religions have phrased the God question. Is creation good? Can reality be trusted? Is being gracious? In some deep level of their personality most men have decided this question one way or another, but until they have the courage to make that decision explicit and face all the implications of such a decision, they will necessarily remain religious adolescents.

There is a fourth substitute for graciousness, and that is what Dr. Martin Marty, in *Youth Considers Do-It-Yourself Religion,* in this series, describes as "religion-in-general," the shallow, superficial, and comforting religious "overlay" which many Americans use to hide from the more difficult and disturbing religious questions. It is a religion that stresses autonomy, self-reliance, self-fulfillment, family happiness, domestic peace, international anti-communism, sexual well-adjustment, and the wonders of the American way of life. It is an affirmation of graciousness of a sort that makes graciousness, indeed the Ultimate Principle of Graciousness, look very much like a middle-class American. It requires little movement toward an omega point and very little confrontation with the problems of suffering and evil, since suffering and evil are viewed as a residue of the past which science, progress, and education can be expected to eliminate in due time. Even the awesome reality of death is covered over with hygienic platitudes. American "religion-in-general" has solved the problem of graciousness by eliminating the problem of evil and converting the world into an extension of an American middle-class suburb. It is an extremely consoling religion and one which most Americans find useful for their own emotional needs. It has nothing to do, of course, with the God of Abraham or the God of Isaac or the God of Jacob, and it has equally little to do with traditional Judaism or Christianity. It is a descendant of two prophetic religions out of which all the prophesy had been squeezed; even the graciousness that is permitted in "religion-in-general" is a graciousness out of which all passion, power, and demonic force has been eliminated. It is really not much of a religion at all, or much of a response to the question of graciousness, and a God who is no longer a Semite warrior or a Great Hangman in the Sky, or even a kindly old father figure, but a well-scrubbed, upper-middle-class suburban professional, is not exactly a God who is likely to arouse much dedication or enmity. One feels inclined to respond to those who say that God is dead by arguing that He is not dead, but in prison in suburbia.

But if the "religion-in-general" response to the God and graciousness question is a shallow, superficial, and impoverished response, the young person should still realize that it is probably the one that will have the greatest temptation for him and the solution for which most of his contemporaries will settle, whether they accept the solution after having traveled the path of total revolt to total compromise or whether it is achieved by a relatively painless passage from childhood conformity to adult conformity.

In conclusion, we can see that the real difficulty the young person must experience in making a conscious, open, and well-thought-out response to the God question is that there are really four confused and overlapping issues: God, graciousness, religion, and church. The graciousness question is the central one and when one has decided this, one has implicitly decided about God and probably about religion, too, though yet another decision has to be made about the church. While these questions are different in their verbal expression, they overlap and obscure one another. They must all be considered both as distinct and as interrelated. The various substitute religions that have been discussed in this chapter are essentially the result of refusing to see either the distinctness or the interrelatedness of the four issues, and more basically, perhaps, of trying to escape from the awesomeness and the terror of the most important question of all: Does life have purpose, goodness, and beauty, or is it all a meaningless charade? The young person who chooses to respond to this issue by pursuing science or progress or revolution or his career or money or power or by professing either a narrow and repressive religious faith or a shallow and optimistic religious faith, has obviously not come to terms with the basic problem, and to the extent that he has not, he is not behaving like a mature human adult.

the resurrection
of God

It has been the purpose of this volume to specify what the basic issue is on the question of whether God is alive or dead. We have striven to eliminate the irrelevancies, the obstacles, the phony issues, the escapes, and the fixations which might stand in the way of a young person taking a cold, hard look at the nature of reality and deciding for himself whether he can accept His graciousness or not. We have warned him in particular of the dangers of yielding to the tendencies of his own psychological background to revolt against his parents and adult society by revolting against God, church, and religion. But we have not attempted to make an argument for or against the graciousness of being, even though we have made some attempt to show how one can, if one chooses for graciousness, break through the difficulties of God talk to conceive of graciousness in such a way that it is relevant to one's life commitments. We have also suggested that for someone raised in the Christian tradition, it is difficult to isolate the question of graciousness from the question of resurrection.

But it would be impossible to obscure the fact that the author of the present volume has a commitment to one side of the issue. This work would not be part of a religious series and would not be written by a clergyman if it were not "prejudiced" in favor of a response affirming graciousness. While we are not attempting to deceive the reader when we say that the major purpose of this book is to insist that the issues be properly stated, it probably has been obvious that there is not much doubt in the mind of the writer how the issue will be decided by most people when it is stripped of the obscurities, the irrelevancies, and the fixations which stand in the way. When maturational progress has been reasonably healthy, when a man has learned at least some modicum of trust from his parents and from his peers of his own sexuality, he is strongly inclined to be an optimist and even to arrive at the rather mad conclusion that even if reality is not graciousness, life is far more pleasant when one makes a commitment to graciousness and lives as though it were.

But such a decision is not one into which people can be argued and we did not intend, in the beginning of the present volume, to argue with anyone. There are all kinds of "proofs" for the existence of God— Aristotle's and St. Thomas's five ways, Anselm's ontological argument, Kant's moral imperative, and the Augustinian-Kirkegaardian argument for man's hunger for the absolute. These various arguments will have greater or lesser degree of plausibility for different personalities. They can even, one supposes, lead to rational assent to the proposition that there is a God; some form of such argumentation is probably necessary as a prelude to faith, though it often seems that those who spend considerable lengths of time agonizing over these preludes never seem to get off them, never seem to work up the courage that it takes to make the leap of faith—either faith of graciousness or faith in malignancy. Faith cannot be demonstrated the way one can demonstrate Newton's law or the truth of the multiplication tables. It is not merely a rational assent, though it may presume a rational assent. Faith is a leap of the total human personality—a commitment of one's person to an ideology and not merely the acceptance by the mind of a series of academic propositions. No one can be argued into faith, though argumentation and reasoning can persuade one that the object of faith is highly probable. Certainty about the commitment, of its very nature, cannot come before the act of commitment and this is true whether one chooses the theistic or the atheistic faith, the faith of graciousness or the faith of malignancy.

Pierre Rousselot, the French Jesuit theologian who was killed in World War I, put his finger on the core problem when he wrote of the "eyes of faith." For Rousselot, the commitment of faith was not only an act of intellectual acceptance, but also an act of love. To illustrate his dynamics, Rousselot pointed out the psychology of love between two human beings. A boy and a girl encounter each other in passing. At first neither sees in the other the kind of traits that each is seeking in a lover, but there is some small bit of attractiveness that holds the attention. Because of this attractiveness each pauses and looks a little more carefully at the other and then, as one considers the other, more attractiveness begins to emerge. This attractiveness, in its turn, reinforces the insight and one begins to discover about the other beauty and goodness that one did not dream was there, and that, indeed in many instances, the other did not even know that she possessed because the lover sees attractive qualities in the beloved. These attractive qualities, which may have existed only inchoately, now begin to grow and flourish. One really knows who the other is only when one sees the other as the beloved one—the one who is the object of one's desires and concerns and affection and love. We only know who another person is when we are committed in love to the other. The eyes of love see far more than the eyes of rationality. It is often said that love is blind, and surely some kinds of youthful infatuation are blind, but mature love is anything but blind. It sees with an instinct and an insight and a clarity that mere rational discussion and observation can never achieve.

According to Rousselot, man's faith in graciousness operates the same way. It is only when he begins to commit himself in love to the graciousness of being that he is able to begin to see now with certainty that being is, in fact, gracious. Or to put the matter more explicitly, it is only when one begins to act as though there were a God and He were relevant that one finally is enabled to believe with conviction that God is present. The leap of a total person in faith is the only way one will ever come to know that the object of faith is truly present. Certainty does not precede love, but rather accompanies it.

Therefore we conclude by saying that the only way to know whether God is alive, with the kind of certainty that cannot be shaken, is to act as if He were. We are not advocating a blind leap, a leap without a consideration of the problems and the arguments that must be faced before the leap; we are merely pointing out that one must eventually leap one way or the other, and that reasoning, argument, and discussion will never produce enough conviction to justify a leap either way. The act of faith in the proposition that God is dead is a mature, if in our judgment, mistaken act. It is a commitment to a reality which the argumentation in this book has accepted as malign. One can perhaps live, even live with some degree of stoic happiness, with such a commitment, but the act of faith in the proposition that God is alive, risen from the tomb once again, is a profession of faith in the goodness, the beauty, the rationality, of reality, and the ultimate triumph, perhaps through man's cooperation, of graciousness over malignancy. Such a commitment brings far more happiness, satisfaction, and joy than does its opposite. This ought to be a fairly persuasive argument that it is the correct leap, and it is the only argument we intend to offer.